Christmas Carol Lyric Book Songs for piano

Table of Contents

Table of Contents

# O Holy Night

O Holy Night!
The stars are brightly shining
It is the night of the dear Savior's birth!
Long lay the world in sin and error pining
Till he appear'd and the soul felt its worth.
A thrill of hope the weary soul rejoices
For yonder breaks a new and glorious morn!
Fall on your knees
Oh hear the angel voices
Oh night divine
Oh night when Christ was born
Oh night divine
Oh night divine
Led by the light of Faith serenely beaming
With glowing hearts by His cradle we stand
So led by light of a star sweetly gleaming
Here come the wise men from Orient land
The King of Kings lay thus in lowly manger
In all our trials born to be our friend
Truly He taught us to love one another
His law is love and His gospel is peace
Chains shall He break for the slave is our brother
And in His name all oppression shall cease
Sweet hymns of joy in grateful chorus raise we,
Let all within us praise His holy name

Silent Night

Silent night, holy night!
All is calm, all is bright.
Round yon Virgin, Mother and Child.
Holy infant so tender and mild,
Sleep in heavenly peace,
Sleep in heavenly peace

Silent night, holy night!
Shepherds quake at the sight.
Glories stream from heaven afar
Heavenly hosts sing Alleluia,
Christ the Savior is born!
Christ the Savior is born

Silent night, holy night!
Son of God love's pure light.
Radiant beams from Thy holy face
With dawn of redeeming grace,
Jesus Lord, at Thy birth
Jesus Lord, at Thy birth

In the Bleak Midwinter

In the bleak mid-winter
Frosty wind made moan;
Earth stood hard as iron,
Water like a stone;
Snow had fallen, snow on snow,
Snow on snow,
In the bleak mid-winter
Long ago.
Our God, heaven cannot hold Him
Nor earth sustain,
Heaven and earth shall flee away
When He comes to reign:
In the bleak mid-winter
A stable-place sufficed
The Lord God Almighty –
Jesus Christ.
Enough for Him, whom Cherubim
Worship night and day,
A breastful of milk
And a mangerful of hay;
Enough for Him, whom Angels
Fall down before,
The ox and ass and camel

Which adore.
Angels and Archangels
May have gathered there,
Cherubim and seraphim
Thronged the air;
But only His Mother
In her maiden bliss
Worshipped the Beloved
With a kiss.

What can I give Him,
Poor as I am?
If I were a Shepherd
I would bring a lamb;
If I were a Wise Man
I would do my part,
Yet what I can I give Him,
Give my heart.

Hark the Herald Angel Sing

Hark! the herald angels sing
Glory to the newborn King
Peace on earth, and mercy mild
God and sinners reconciled
Joyful, all ye nations, rise
Join the triumph of the skies
With th' angelic host proclaim
Christ is born in Bethlehem
Har, the herald angels sing
Glory to the newborn King
Hail, the heav'n-born Prince of peace
Hail! the Son of Righteousness
Light and life to all he brings
Risen with healing in his wings
Mild he lays his glory by
Born that man no more may die
Born to raise the some of earth
Born to give them second birth

Hark! the herald angels sing
Glory to the newborn King
Hark, the herald angels sing
Glory to the newborn King
Peace on earth, and mercy mild
God and sinners reconciled
Joyful, all ye nations, rise
Join the triumph of the skies
With th' angelic host proclaim
Christ is born in Bethlehem
Hark, the herald angels sing
Glory to the newborn King

O Come, All Ye Faithful

O come, all ye faithful, joyful and
triumphant!
O come ye, O come ye, to Bethlehem
Come and behold Him
Born the King of Angels
O come, let us adore Him
O come, let us adore Him
O come, let us adore Him
Christ the Lord!
God of God, Light of Light
Lo, He abhors not the Virgin's womb
Very God
Begotten, not created
O come, let us adore Him
O come, let us adore Him
O come, let us adore Him
Christ the Lord!

Sing, choirs of angels, sing
in exultation
Sing, all ye citizens of
heaven above!
Glory to God
All glory in the highest
O come, let us adore Him
O come, let us adore Him
O come, let us adore Him
Christ the Lord!
Yea, Lord, we greet Thee,
born this happy morning
Jesus, to Thee be glory
given
Word of the Father
Now in flesh appearing
O come, let us adore Him
O come, let us adore Him
O come, let us adore Him
Christ the Lord!

O Little Town of Bethlehem

Oh little town of Bethlehem, how still we see thee lie

Above thy deep and dreamless sleep the silent stars go b

Yet in thy dark streets shineth, the everlasting light

The hopes and fears of all the years are met in thee tonight.

For Christ is born of Mary, and gathered all above

While mortals sleep the angels keep their watch of wondering love

Oh morning stars together, proclaim thy holy birth.

And praises sing to God the king, and peace to men on earth.

Oh little town of Bethlehem, how still we see thee lie

Above thy deep and dreamless sleep the silent stars go b

Yet in thy dark streets shineth, the everlasting light

The hopes and fears of all the years are met in thee tonight.

Joy to the World

Joy to the world, the Lord has come
Let earth receive her King
Let every heart prepare Him room
And heaven and nature sing, and heaven and
nature sing
And heaven, and heaven and nature sing

Joy to the world, the Savior reigns
Let men their songs employ
While fields and floods, rocks, hills, and plains
Repeat the sounding joy, repeat the sounding
joy
Repeat, repeat the sounding joy
No more let sins and sorrows grow
Nor thorns infest the ground
He comes to make His blessings flow
Far as the curse is found, far as the curse is
found
Far as, far as the curse is found

Joy to the World

He rules the world with truth and grace
And makes the nations prove (And makes
the nations prove)
And glories of His righteousness
And wonders of His love
And wonders of His love
And wonders of His love
And wonders, wonders of His love
And wonders, wonders of His love
Joy to the world then we sing
Let the earth receive her King!
Joy to the world then we sing
Let the angel voices ring

Away in a Manger

Away in a manger
No crib for a bed
The little Lord Jesus
Laid down His sweet head
The stars in the bright sky
Looked down where He lay
The little Lord Jesus
Asleep on the hay
The cattle are lowing
The Baby awakes
But little Lord Jesus
No crying He makes
I love You, Lord Jesus
Look down from the sky
And stay by my side
Until morning is nigh
Be near me, Lord Jesus
I ask You to stay
Close by me forever
And love me I pray
Bless all the dear children
In Your tender care
And fit us for heaven
To live with You there

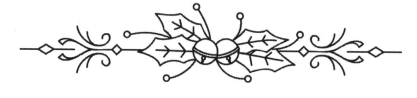

The First Noel

Noel, Noel

Noel, Noel

The First Noel, the Angels did say

Was to certain poor shepherds in fields as they lay

In fields where they lay keeping their sheep

On a cold winter's night that was so deep

Noel, Noel, Noel, Noel

Born is the King of Israel!

Noel, Noel

Noel, Noel

They looked up and saw a star

Shining in the East beyond them far

And to the earth it gave great light

And so it continued both day and night

Noel, Noel

Noel, Noel

Noel, Noel

Noel, Noel

Noel, Noel

Noel, Noel

Born is the King of Israel!

Noel, Noel, Noel, Noel

Born is the King of Israel!

Born is the King of Israel!

Noel, Noel

Noel, Noel

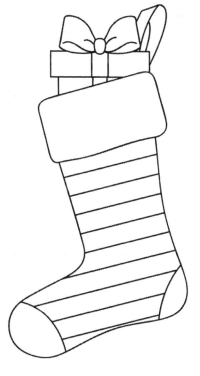

Go Tell It on the Mountain

Go, tell it on the mountain
Over the hills and everywhere
Go, tell it on the mountain
That Jesus Christ is born
While shepherds kept their watching
O'er silent flocks by night
Behold throughout the heavens
There shone a Holy light
Go, tell it on the mountain
Over the hills and everywhere
Go, tell it on the mountain
That Jesus Christ is born
The shepherds feared and trembled
When, lo! Above the Earth
Rang out the angel chorus
That hailed our Savior's birth
Go, tell it on the mountain
Over the hills and everywhere

Go, tell it on the mountain
That Jesus Christ is born
Down in a lowly manger
Our humble Christ was born
And brought us all salvation
That blessed Christmas morn
Go, tell it on the mountain
Over the hills and everywhere
Go, tell it on the mountain
That Jesus Christ is born
That Jesus Christ is born

Jingle Bells

Dashing through the snow
In a one-horse open sleigh,
O'er the fields we go,
Laughing all the way.
Bells on bob-tails ring,
Making spirits bright.
What fun it is to ride and sing
A sleighing song tonight, oh!
Jingle bells, jingle bells,
Jingle all the way.
Oh what fun it is to ride
In a one-horse open sleigh, hey!
Jingle bells, jingle bells,
Jingle all the way.
Oh what fun it is to ride,
In a one-horse open sleigh.

Now the ground is white,
Go it while you're young.
Take the girls tonight,
Sing this sleighing song.
Get a bobtailed bay,
Two forty for his speed,
And hitch him to an open sleigh
And you will take the lead.
Oh, jingle bells, jingle bells,
Jingle all the way.
Oh! what fun it is to ride,
In a one-horse open sleigh, hey
Jingle bells, jingle bells,
Jingle all the way.
Oh! what fun it is to ride,
In a one-horse open sleigh,
Oh, what fun it is to ride
In one horse open sleigh!

We Wish You a Merry Christmas

We wish you a merry Christmas
We wish you a merry Christmas
We wish you a merry Christmas and a happy new year
Good tidings we bring to you and your kin
We wish you a merry Christmas and a happy new year
Oh, bring us some figgy pudding
Oh, bring us some figgy pudding
Oh, bring us some figgy pudding
And bring it right here
Good tidings we bring to you and your kin
We wish you a merry Christmas and a happy new year
We won't go until we get some
We won't go until we get some
We won't go until we get some
So bring it right here
Good tidings we bring to you and your kin
We wish you a merry Christmas and a happy new year
We all like our figgy pudding
We all like our figgy pudding
We all like our figgy pudding
With all its good cheers
Good tidings we bring to you and your kin
We wish you a merry Christmas and a happy new year
We wish you a merry Christmas
We wish you a merry Christmas
We wish you a merry Christmas and a happy new year

O Christmas Tree

O Christmas Tree, O Christmas tree,
How lovely are your branches!
O Christmas Tree, O Christmas tree,
How lovely are your branches!
Not only green in summer's heat,
But also winter's snow and sleet.
O Christmas tree, O Christmas tree,
How lovely are your branches!
O Christmas Tree, O Christmas tree,
Of all the trees most lovely;
O Christmas Tree, O Christmas tree,
Of all the trees most lovely.
Each year you bring to us delight
With brightly shining Christmas light!
O Christmas Tree, O Christmas tree,
Of all the trees most lovely.
O Christmas Tree, O Christmas tree,
We learn from all your beauty;
O Christmas Tree, O Christmas tree,
We learn from all your beauty.
Your bright green leaves with festive cheer,
Give hope and strength throughout the year.
O Christmas Tree, O Christmas tree,
We learn from all your beauty

Angels We Have Heard on High

Angels we have heard on high
Sweetly singing o'er the plains
And the mountains in reply
Echoing their joyous strains
Angels we have heard on high
Sweetly, sweetly through the night
And the mountains in reply
Echoing their brief delight
Gloria, in excelsis Deo
Gloria, in excelsis Deo
Shepherds, why this jubilee?
Why your joyous strains prolong?
What the gladsome tidings be
Which inspire your heavenly song?
Gloria, in excelsis Deo
Gloria, in excelsis Deo

Angels We Have Heard on High

Come to Bethlehem and see
Him whose birth the angels sing,
Come, adore on bended knee,
Christ the Lord, the newborn King.
Gloria, in excelsis Deo
Gloria, in excelsis Deo
Yeah
Gloria, in excelsis Deo
Angels we have heard
Angels we have heard on high
Angels we have heard, oh
Angels we have heard on high
Angels we have heard on high
Angels we have heard on high
In excelsis Deo

Bring a torch, Jeanette, Isabella

Bring a torch, Jeanette, Isabella
Bring a torch, to the cradle run!
It is Jesus, good folk of the village;
Christ is born and Mary's calling;
Ah! ah! beautiful is the Mother
Ah! ah! beautiful is her Son!
It is wrong when the Child is sleeping
It is wrong to talk so loud;
Silence, all, as you gather around.
Lest your noise should waken Jesus.
Hush! hush! see how fast He slumbers!
Hush! hush! see how fast He sleeps!
Hasten now, good folk of the village;
Hasten now the Christ Child to see.
You will find Him asleep in the manger;
Quietly come and whisper softly,
Hush! hush! Peacefully now He slumbers.
Hush! hush! Peacefully now He sleeps.
Softly to the little stable.
Softly for a moment come;
Look and see how charming is Jesus
How He is white, His cheeks are rosy!
Hush! hush! see how the Child is sleeping;
Hush! hush! see how He smiles in his dreams.

Coventry Carol

Lullay, thou little tiny child
Sleep well, lully, lullay
And smile in dreaming, little one
Sleep well, lully, lullay
Oh sisters two, what may we do
To preserve on this day
This poor youngling for whom we sing
Sleep well, lully, lullay
Farewell, lully, lullay
Herod the king in his raging
Set forth upon this day
By his decree, no life spare thee
All children young to slay
All children young to slay
Then woe is me, poor child, for thee
And ever mourn and say
For thy parting, neither say nor sing
Farewell, lully, lullay
Farewell, lully, lullay
And when the stars fill darkened skies
In their far venture, stay
And smile as dreaming, little one
Farewell, lully, lullay
Dream now, lully, lullay

Here We Come a Caroling

Here we come a-caroling,
Among the leaves so green!
Here we coma a-wandering,
So fair to be seen!
Love and joy come to you,
And to you glad Christmas too,
And God bless you and send you,
A Happy New Year,
And God send you a Happy New Year!
We are not daily beggars,
That go from door to door!
But we are friendly neighbours,
Whom you have seen before!
Love and joy come to you,
And to you glad Christmas too,
And God bless you and send you,
A Happy New Year,
And God send you a Happy New Year!
We wish you a Merry Christmas,
We wish you a Merry Christmas,
We wish you a Merry Christmas,
And a Happy New Year!

Here We Come a Caroling

Good tidings to you,
Wherever you are,
Good tidings for Christmas,
And a Happy New Year!
We wish you a Merry Christmas,
We wish you a Merry Christmas,
We wish you a Merry Christmas,
And a Happy New Year!
We wish you a Merry Christmas,
We wish you a Merry Christmas,
We wish you a Merry Christmas,
And a Happy New Year

We Three Kings

We three kings of Orient are
Bearing gifts we traverse afar
Field and fountain, moor and
mountain
Following yonder star
We three kings, we three kings
Born a king on Bethlehem's plain
Gold I bring to crown Him again
King forever, ceasing never
Over us all to reign
Oh, star of wonder, star of night
Star with royal beauty bright
Westward leading, still proceeding
Guide us to thy perfect light
We three kings, we three kings
Myrrh is mine, it's bitter perfume
Breaths a life of gathering gloom
Sorrowing, sighing, bleeding dying
Sealed in the stone-cold tomb

We Three Kings

Oh, star of wonder, star of night
Star with royal beauty bright
Westward leading, still proceeding
Guide us to thy perfect light
Star of wonder, star of night
Star with royal beauty bright
Westward leading, still proceeding
Guide us to thy perfect light
We three kings, we three kings
We three kings, we three kings
We three kings, we three kings
We three kings, we three kings
We three kings, we three kings

The twelve days of christmas

On the first day of Christmas, my true love sent to me A partridge in a pear tree.

On the second day of Christmas, my true love sent to me Two turtle doves, And a partridge in a pear tree.

On the third day of Christmas, my true love sent to me Three French hens, Two turtle doves, And a partridge in a pear tree.

On the fourth day of Christmas, my true love sent to me Four calling birds, Three French hens, Two turtle doves, And a partridge in a pear tree.

On the fifth day of Christmas, my true love sent to me Five golden rings, Four calling birds, Three French hens, Two turtle doves, And a partridge in a pear tree.

On the sixth day of Christmas, my true love sent to me Six geese a-laying, Five golden rings, Four calling birds, Three French hens, Two turtle doves, And a partridge in a pear tree.

On the seventh day of Christmas, my true love sent to me Seven swans a-swimming, Six geese a-laying, Five golden rings, Four calling birds, Three French hens, Two turtle doves, And a partridge in a pear tree.

On the eighth day of Christmas, my true love sent to me Eight maids a-milking, Seven swans a-swimming, Six geese a-laying, Five golden rings, Four calling birds, Three French hens, Two turtle doves, And a partridge in a pear tree.

The twelve days of christmas

On the ninth day of Christmas, my true love sent to me Nine ladies dancing, Eight maids a-milking, Seven swans a-swimming, Six geese a-laying, Five golden rings, Four calling birds, Three French hens, Two turtle doves, And a partridge in a pear tree.

On the tenth day of Christmas, my true love sent to me Ten lords a-leaping, Nine ladies dancing, Eight maids a-milking, Seven swans a-swimming, Six geese a-laying, Five golden rings, Four calling birds, Three French hens, Two turtle doves, And a partridge in a pear tree.

On the eleventh day of Christmas, my true love sent to me Eleven pipers piping, Ten lords a-leaping, Nine ladies dancing, Eight maids a-milking, Seven swans a-swimming, Six geese a-laying, Five golden rings, Four calling birds, Three French hens, Two turtle doves, And a partridge in a pear tree.

On the twelfth day of Christmas, my true love sent to me Twelve drummers drumming, Eleven pipers piping, Ten lords a-leaping, Nine ladies dancing, Eight maids a-milking, Seven swans a-swimming, Six geese a-laying, Five golden rings, Four calling birds, Three French hens, Two turtle doves, And a partridge in a pear tree!

Toyland

Toyland, toyland
Little girl and boy land
While you dwell within it
You are ever happy there
Childhood's joy land
Mystic merry toyland
Once you pass its borders
You can ne'er return again
When you've grown up, my dears
And are as old as I
You'll laugh and ponder on the years
That roll so swiftly by, my dears
That roll so swiftly by
Childhood's joy land
Mystic merry toyland
Once you pass its borders
You can ne'er return again

I Heard the Bells on Christmas Day

I heard the bells on Christmas day
Their old familiar carols play
And mild and sweet their songs repeat
Of peace on Earth, good will to men
And the bells are ringing (peace on Earth)
Like a choir they're singing (peace on Earth)
In my heart I hear them (peace on Earth)
Peace on Earth, good will to men
And in despair I bowed my head
"There is no peace on Earth, " I said
For hate is strong and mocks the song
Of peace on Earth, good will to men
But the bells are ringing (peace on Earth)
Like a choir singing (peace on Earth)
Does anybody hear them? (Peace on Earth)
Peace on Earth, good will to men
Then rang the bells more loud and deep
God is not dead, nor doth He sleep
(Peace on Earth)
(Peace on Earth)

I Heard the Bells on Christmas Day

The wrong shall fail, the right prevail

With peace on Earth, good will to men

Then ringing, singing on its way

The world revolved from night to day

A voice, a chime, a chant sublime

Of peace on Earth, good will to men

And the bells, they're ringing (peace on Earth)

Like a choir they're singing (peace on Earth)

And with our hearts, we'll hear them (peace on Earth)

Peace on Earth, good will to men

Do you hear the bells, they're ringing? (Peace on Earth)

The light, the angels singing (peace on Earth)

Open up your heart and hear them (peace on Earth)

Peace on Earth, good will to men

Peace on Earth

Peace on Earth

Peace on Earth, good will to men

O come, O come, Emmanuel

O come, O come, Emmanuel,
And ransom captive Israel,
That mourns in lonely exile here,
Until the Son of God appear.
Rejoice! Rejoice! Emmanuel
Shall come to thee, O Israel.
O come, Thou Rod of Jesse, free
Thine own from Satan's tyranny;
From depths of hell Thy people save,
And give them victory o'er the grave.
Rejoice! Rejoice! Emmanuel
Shall come to thee, O Israel.

O come, Thou Dayspring, from on high,
And cheer us by Thy drawing nigh;
Disperse the gloomy clouds of night,
And death's dark shadows put to flight.
Rejoice! Rejoice! Emmanuel
Shall come to thee, O Israel.

O come, O come, Emmanuel

O come, Thou Key of David, come
And open wide our heav'nly home;
Make safe the way that leads on high,
And close the path to misery.
Rejoice! Rejoice! Emmanuel
Shall come to thee, O Israel.

O come, Adonai, Lord of might,
Who to Thy tribes, on Sinai's height,
In ancient times didst give the law
In cloud and majesty and awe.
Rejoice! Rejoice! Emmanuel
Shall come to thee, O Israel

Once in Royal David's City

Once in royal Davids city,
Stood a lowly cattle shed,
Where a mother laid her Baby,
In a manger for His bed:
Mary was that mother mild,
Jesus Christ, her little Child.
He came down to earth from heaven,
Who is God and Lord of all,
And His shelter was a stable,
And His cradle was a stall:
With the poor, and mean, and lowly,
Lived on earth our Saviour holy.
For He is our childhood's pattern;
Day by day, like us, He grew;
He was little, weak, and helpless,
Tears and smiles, like us He knew;
And He cares when we are sad,
And he shares when we are glad.
And our eyes at last shall see Him,
Through His own redeeming love;
For that Child so dear and gentle,
Is our Lord in heaven above:
And He leads His children on,
To the place where He is gone.

Deck the Halls

Deck the halls with boughs of holly, Fa la la la la la la la la!

'Tis the season to be jolly, Fa la la la la la la la la!
Don we now our gay apparel, Fa la la la la la la la la!
Troll the ancient Yuletide carol, Fa la la la la la la la la!

See the blazing yule before us, Fa la la la la la la la la!
Strike the harp and join the chorus, Fa la la la la la la la la!

Follow me in merry measure, Fa la la la la la la la la!
While I tell of Yuletide treasure, Fa la la la la la la la la!

Fast away the old year passes, Fa la la la la la la la la!
Hail the new, ye lads and lasses, Fa la la la la la la la la!
Sing we joyous all together! Fa la la la la la la la la!
Heedless of the wind and weather, Fa la la la la la la la la!

What Child Is This?

What child is this
Who lay to rest
On Mary's lap is sleeping
Whom angels greet with anthems sweet
While shepherds watch are keeping
So bring him incense, gold and myrrh
Come peasant king to own him
The King of Kings salvation brings
Let loving hearts enthrone him
This, this is Christ the King
Whom shepherds guard and angels sing
Haste, haste to bring him laud
The Babe, the Son of Mary
O raise, raise a song on high
His mother sings a lullaby
Joy, oh joy for Christ is born
The Babe, the son of Mary
This, this is Christ the King
Whom shepherds guard and angels sing
Haste, haste to bring him laud
The Babe, the Son of Mary

What Child Is This?

What child
Is this (is this)
Who lay (who lay)
To rest (to rest)
On Mary's lap (lap)
On Mary's lap he is sleeping
This, this is Christ the King
Whom shepherds guard and angels sing
Haste, haste to bring him laud
The Babe
The Son
Of Mary
The Babe, the Son of Mary
The Son of Mary

Mary, did you know?

Mary, did you know that your baby boy would one day walk on water?

Mary, did you know that your baby boy would save our sons and daughters?

Did you know that your baby boy has come to make you new?

This child that you've delivered, will soon deliver you. Mary, did you know that your baby boy will give sight to a blind man?

Mary, did you know that your baby boy will calm a storm with his hand?

Did you know that your baby boy has walked where angels trod?

When you kiss your little baby, you kissed the face of God.

Mary, did you know?

Mary, did you know, Mary did you know, Mary did you know...

The blind will see, the deaf will hear and the dead will live again.

The lame will leap, the dumb will speak, the praises of the lamb.

Mary, did you know that your baby boy is Lord of all creation?

Mary, did you know that your baby boy will one day rule the nations?

Did you know that your baby boy is heaven's perfect Lamb?

That sleeping child you're holding is the great I am. Mary, did you know,

Mary, did you know,

Mary, did you know...

Mary, did you know...

Jolly Old St. Nicholas

Jolly old St. Nicholas
Lean your ear this way
Don't you tell a single soul
What I'm going to say
Christmas Eve is coming soon
Now, you dear old man
Whisper what you'll bring to me
Tell me if you can

When the clock is striking twelve
When I'm fast asleep
Down the chimney broad and black
With your pack you'll creep
All the stockings you will find
Hanging in a row
Mine will be the shortest one
You'll be sure to know

What's it gonna be, Santa
Underneath the tree, Santa
What's it gonna be, Santa
Be this for me
Jolly old St. Nicholas
Now you dear old man
Whisper what you'll bring to me
Tell me if you can

Jolly Old St. Nicholas

What's it gonna be, Santa
Underneath the tree, Santa
What's it gonna be, Santa
Be this for me
Jason wants a Fender bass
Walt a saxophone
Lee, he needs a flugelhorn
Jimmy, a trombone
Robert wants a baby grand
Bill, a new B3
Tris, he wants a dolly, but
What are you gonna bring to me, Santa?
What's it gonna be, Santa
Underneath the tree, Santa
What's it gonna be, Santa
Be this
What's it gonna be, Santa
Underneath the tree, Santa
What's it gonna be, Santa
Be this for me
How about a shiny electric guitar, Santa?

Auld Lang Syne

Should auld acquaintance be forgot
And never brought to mind?
Should auld acquaintance be forgot
And days of auld lang syne?
For auld lang syne, my dear
For auld lang syne
We'll tak a cup o' kindness yet
For days of auld lang syne
We twa hae run about the braes
And pu'd the gowans fine
But we've wander'd mony a weary fit
Sin days of auld lang syne
We twa hae paidl'd i' the burn
Frae morning sun till dine
But seas between us braid hae roar'd
Sin days of auld lang syne
For auld lang syne, my dear
For auld lang syne
We'll tak a cup o' kindness yet
For days of auld lang syne

Auld Lang Syne

And surely ye'll be your pint-stowp
And surely I'll be mine
And we'll tak a cup o' kindness yet
For auld lang syne
And there's a hand, my trusty fiere
And gie's a hand o' thine
And we'll tak a right gude-willy waught
For auld lang syne
For auld lang syne, my dear
For auld lang syne
We'll tak a cup o' kindness yet
For auld lang syne
For auld lang syne, my dear
For auld lang syne
We'll tak a cup o' kindness yet
For auld lang syne

The Holly and the Ivy

The holly and the ivy,
When they are both full grown,
Of all trees that are in the wood,
The holly bears the crown
O, the rising of the sun,
And the running of the deer
The playing of the merry organ,
The holly bears a blossom,
As white as lily flow'r,
And Mary bore sweet Jesus Christ,
To be our dear Saviour
O, the rising of the sun,
And the running of the deer
The playing of the merry organ,
The holly bears a berry,
As red as any blood,
And Mary bore sweet Jesus Christ,
To do poor sinners good
O, the rising of the sun,
And the running of the deer
The playing of the merry organ,
The holly bears a prickle,
As sharp as any thorn,
And Mary bore sweet Jesus Christ,
On Christmas Day in the morn

The Holly and the Ivy

O, the rising of the sun,
And the running of the deer
The playing of the merry organ,
The holly bears a bark,
As bitter as the gall,
And Mary bore sweet Jesus Christ,
For to redeem us all
O, the rising of the sun,
And the running of the deer
The playing of the merry organ,
The holly and the ivy,
When they are both full grown,
Of all trees that are in the wood,
The holly bears the crown
O, the rising of the sun,
And the running of the deer
The playing of the merry organ,

It Came Upon a Midnight Clear

It came upon a midnight clear
That glorious song of old
From angels bending near the earth
To touch their harps of gold
Peace on the earth, good will to men
From heaven's all gracious King
The world in solemn stillness lay
To hear the angels sing
Still through the cloven skies they come
With peaceful wings unfurled
And still their heavenly music floats
O'er all the weary world
Above its sad and lowly plains
They bend on hovering wing
And ever o'er its Babel sounds
The blessed angels sing
All ye beneath life's crushing load
Whose forms are bending low
Who toil along the climbing way
With painful steps and slow
Look now for glad and golden hours
Come swiftly on the wing
O rest beside the weary road
And hear the angels sing
And hear the angels sing

Merry Christmas caroling

Visit also our author page and see other our products

Made in the USA
Middletown, DE
02 November 2022

13957706R00029